The Body Remembers

A Soft Return to the Light Within

blanche johanna

© 2025 blanche johanna

All rights reserved.

No part of this publication may be reproduced, stored in a retrieval system, or transmitted in any form or by any means, electronic, mechanical, photocopying, recording, or otherwise, without the prior written permission of the author.

This book is a spiritual and creative transmission intended to support personal and collective awakening. All guidance and reflections are shared from the author's lived and intuitive experience and are not intended as a substitute for professional advice.

The Body Remembers™ is a trademark of blanche johanna. All rights reserved.

ISBN: 978-1-7641285-6-8

www.blanchejohanna.com

Prelude

the hush before touch

I have come here to remember,
not only with my mind,
not only with the star of my soul,
but with my skin, my breath, my trembling hands.

I have come to let the sacred find me,
through the ache in my shoulders,
the gentle pulse in my throat,
the tender fold of my belly.

I am here to remember that my body is not separate
from the light,
it is not a thing to be transcended or conquered,
it is the holy animal of my becoming,
the living testament of all I have ever loved.

So I stand now in this quiet threshold,
between forgetting and soft knowing,
and I invite the first breath to enter me again,
to move through the corridors of my bones,
to whisper into the marrow,
you are made of light.

let this be the soft return,
the slow opening of every cell,
to the truth that was never lost,
only waiting to be felt.

here, in this hush before touch,
the body remembers itself,
and everything begins anew.

Contents

1. The Skin Knows

2. Bones of Light

3. The Blood Carries Songs

4. Breath as Return

5. The Ache is a Portal

6. Softening into Trust

7. A Dance with the Invisible

8. The Holy Animal

9. The Body Remembers

Chapter One

The Skin Knows

Before you ever spoke a word, before your lungs learned the rhythm of this world, your skin was already knowing.

It knows the hush of midnight air across your shoulders, the bite of winter, the hum of summer heat sinking into your chest. It knows how to drink sunlight without effort, to ripple with goosebumps at a single breeze.

Your skin is the first remembrance of contact. It is where the body learned the language of belonging. Long before the mind could label safe or unsafe, right or wrong, your skin simply received.

It holds the imprint of every embrace, the tender ones that settled like balm, and the ones that left you trembling in the dark. It keeps the faint ghosts of hands that soothed you, as well as the shadow of hands that did not. It remembers the times you pulled away, the times you longed to be touched and were not, the times you learned to stand rigid and small.

And yet, in all of this, your skin never turned to stone. Even now, it shivers with life. It expands when warmth draws near, contracts when cold approaches, opens in quiet delight under a gentle palm.

It does not hold grudges. It does not keep score. It simply remembers, everything.

Place your hands upon your own body. Let your palms rest lightly against the curve of your shoulder, your belly, your heart. Feel how your skin receives even your own touch.

There is a softness here that asks nothing of you. It only wants to remember the simple miracle of contact: the subtle electricity that says *I am here, I am alive, I belong to this moment.*

Your skin knows you are not separate. It stands as a living veil, not to keep the world out, but to let it enter you in a thousand tiny ways.

This is the first place the light comes home, not through thought or reason, but through the quiet language of sensation.

In this way, the body remembers everything, and still says yes. It softens. It opens. It invites life back in, over and over, no matter how many times it was hurt.

Let your skin have this yes. Let it breathe again. In that tender opening, the ancient memory of wholeness stirs, and you begin to return.

Chapter Two

Bones of Light

Long before you learned to stand, before your feet pressed into the earth with any certainty, your bones were already humming.

They are more than structure. More than silent pillars holding your shape. Your bones are archives, living crystalline libraries that remember the weight of countless worlds.

Each curve of rib, each hollow of pelvis, each length of spine holds stories older than this lifetime. They carry echoes of the gravity of other planets, the gentle pull of unfamiliar moons, the soft crush of grass beneath feet that are not these feet.

Your bones are forged from stardust, not as poetry, but as the deepest biological truth. They know the burn of solar winds, the hush of drifting through the dark between galaxies. They remember collisions and caresses, the building and breaking of countless forms.

If you are quiet enough, you might feel them sigh. In the stillness, a subtle vibration moves through your marrow, a song that predates language. It speaks not in words, but in pulses, reminding you that you have stood up from dust and laid yourself down again more times than you could ever count.

Your bones also hold the gentle burdens of lineage. The genetic rivers of those who came before you flow here, pooling in the delicate chambers of your skeleton. The laugh lines etched in ancestors' faces, the stooped shoulders of grief long carried, the strong jaws of survival. All of it lives here, shaped into the very architecture that keeps you upright.

And yet beyond the inherited, beyond the human, your bones carry the original blueprint of light. Before any blood moved through them, before any ache bent them, they were patterned from the codes of creation itself.

Touch your wrist now, or press your fingers to the jut of your collarbone. Feel how solid it is. And yet inside, there is a luminous emptiness, a quiet field where light rests in tender spirals.

This is not imagination. It is the truth your cells have always known. Your bones are lanterns, delicate cages of radiance. They hold not just your history, but your foreverness.

So let them remember. Let them breathe. Trust that even when you feel weary, when your body aches and the world presses too close, there is something inside you that cannot be crushed.

Because beneath the skin, beneath the stories, beneath even the flowing rivers of blood, there is a cathedral of light.
And it is singing your name, over and over, until you remember you were never only flesh.

You are the sacred architecture of remembrance itself. And in this moment, your bones glow with the truth of it.

Chapter Three

The Blood Carries Songs

Before you ever heard music with your ears, your blood was already singing.

It moves through you with a rhythm older than your heartbeat, older than any breath you've taken. It is a river of memory, a crimson thread that weaves together what is human, what is cosmic, what is eternal.

Your blood carries the songs of your ancestors. Not just their wounds and worries, but their laughter, their tender moments of wonder, their quiet triumphs that no history ever recorded. Each cell is imprinted with tiny signatures of those who came before, whispering through you in pulses and tides.

But beyond the lineage of this earth, your blood holds melodies from places far beyond this sky. It remembers the vibration of stars that no longer burn, the hush of nebulae where your essence once drifted, gathering stories to pour into form.

When you close your eyes and feel the soft thrum beneath your skin, you are not simply alive, you are a vessel of songs so ancient they have no words. They move in patterns, in luminous geometries, in gentle codes that unfold only when you are still enough to listen.

Your blood is a library of becoming. It carries the blueprint of your body, yes, but also the subtle map of how light wished to express itself through matter. Every swirl in your fingertips, every fleck of colour in your eyes, every curve of muscle was first dreamt by this river moving inside you.

It is also where the ache lives. The ache for home, for union, for remembrance. Sometimes it pulses so strongly it feels like longing itself is coursing through your veins. But even this is holy. For it means the songs are waking up, stirring the old codes that tell you: you have never been only human.

Press your hand to your heart. Feel how the blood greets you, tender and unhurried. It does not ask you to understand it. It only wants you to trust its song.

Because in the end, it is through this river that the light learns to dance in colour and warmth. It is through this river that you remember you are not merely carrying life, you are life, in motion, luminous, ancient, ever singing itself into form.

Let it sing. Let it guide you back, note by note, to the truth that has always lived quietly within you.

Chapter Four

Breath as Return

Long before language, before even the shaping of bodies into separate forms, there was breath.

It is the first rhythm, the silent tide that moves through all creation. Breath is how light learned to dance, rising and falling, expanding and drawing back, giving itself shape through the gentle motion of being.

In you, it is both ancient and newborn. Each inhale is a return to the first pulse that ever rippled through the vastness, the moment when nothing became something. Each exhale is a surrender, a soft undoing back into the endless field that holds all things.

Your breath remembers this. It does not belong to you; it moves through you. It is the quiet bridge between what is seen and unseen, what is flesh and what is pure luminous knowing.

When you breathe with presence, when you allow the air to fill you without rush or grasping, you open the door for the oldest memory to enter. The memory of being held by something vast and tender, long before there was any name for safety.

Your breath carries codes of home. Not the place you were born into this life, but the greater home, the original belonging that predates all incarnation. Each slow, conscious inhale pulls strands of that memory back through your chest, reminding your cells how to trust.

It is here that much healing happens without effort. Because when you breathe fully, the light moves more easily. It weaves through the rivers of blood, through the lattice of bone, through the shimmering field around your body. It unravels small knots of fear and softens old contractions that once protected you, but no longer need to.

Rest your hand on your belly. Feel how it rises to meet the air, how it falls to let it go. This simple motion is a sacred dance, the universe moving in you, through you, as you.

Let it be gentle. Let it be enough. In these quiet breaths, your body remembers it was never apart from the source of all light.

Here, in this humble act of drawing air, you come home again. And again. And again.

Chapter Five

The Ache is a Portal

There is a tender ache that lives beneath your ribs. It does not always announce itself with pain; often it arrives as a hush, a subtle emptiness that stretches through your chest when the world grows quiet.

This ache is not a flaw. It is not something to fix or banish. It is a doorway. A soft threshold into the deeper chambers of your being.

Long before this life, before the forming of hands and heart and name, you knew yourself as part of a vast field of light. There was no need, no reaching, no longing, only the quiet hum of wholeness, the joy of existing in seamless unity.

When your essence chose to journey into form, to scatter into countless bodies across time and space, it was an act of wonder. A sacred exploration. But it also meant tasting separation, learning the delicate gravity of wanting.

The ache you feel is not only for people or places. It is the body remembering the moment it stepped slightly apart from the endless light, just to see itself anew. It is the echo of your soul's own tender choice to experience reunion by first knowing distance.

When you sit with this ache, when you do not rush to fill it or silence it, something miraculous happens. The portal opens. The light that waits just beyond the edges of your awareness pours through the quiet hollow, meeting you in the space you thought was empty.

Let your hand rest there now, at the centre of your chest. Breathe into the ache without trying to mend it. Feel how it pulses with its own secret knowing.

This is not loneliness. It is a call. A remembering. A gentle thread that tugs you back toward the wholeness that never actually left you.

In this way, the ache becomes a guide. A soft opening through which light can return, more vivid for the journey, more precious for having once seemed lost.

Trust it. Trust the ache. It is your oldest map home.

Chapter Six

Softening into Trust

Your body was never built for constant bracing. It did not come here to live clenched, breath shallow, shoulders tight around a heart that only longs to open.

It came here to be soft. To yield. To trust the ground enough to rest its weight.

There are reasons you learned to tighten. Moments that carved caution into your muscles, that taught your breath to stay high and quick so it could flee at the first hint of harm. These were not failures. They were tender wisdoms, shaped to keep you safe when safety felt scarce.

But now the light is moving differently. It presses gently at the edges of your guard, asking if it might come closer. Not to shatter your defences, but to remind you how it feels to let warmth reach all the way in.

Softening is not the same as surrendering to harm. It is not abandoning discernment or boundaries. It is simply choosing not to armour against the very love you crave.

Place your hands on your belly, feel how it rises when you breathe. Let it be full. Let it spill slightly outward. Notice how the earth beneath you still holds, how nothing breaks when you stop holding yourself so tightly.

This is trust. Not a concept, but an embodied remembering. That you can be vulnerable and still safe. That you can let go, even a little, and not disappear.

Each time you soften, even by a fraction, your nervous system unravels an old knot. Each time you breathe fully, you teach your body that it is allowed to be here, unguarded, alive, receptive to the quiet rivers of light moving toward you.

This is how the deeper codes awaken. Not through force or striving, but through gentle allowance. Through a sigh that travels deeper into your belly than you thought possible. Through a heart that dares to beat unshielded, just for a moment longer.

And in that moment, something ancient stirs. The body remembers how to trust the light it was born from. And for a breath, or maybe forever, you are home inside your own skin.

Chapter Seven

A Dance with the Invisible

Not all knowing comes through sight. Not all touch leaves a mark upon the skin. Much of what shapes you happens in the quiet exchange between your body and the unseen.

You are surrounded by fields of subtle intelligence, rivers of energy that move through and around you even when your eyes cannot trace them. Each breath draws these currents closer. Each sigh releases something back into the delicate weave.

Your body is not blind to this. It senses the invisible in countless tiny ways. The hairs that rise along your neck, the shiver that passes through your shoulders without cause, the sudden warmth that blooms in your chest when no sun is near.

This is your deeper self communing with what cannot be measured. It is your cells listening to the hum of the universe, adjusting, attuning, remembering how to belong to something infinitely larger.

When you sit quietly, you might feel it: a subtle press against your skin, a gentle flutter through your chest, as if unseen hands are brushing against the edges of your field. This is not imagination. It is the body recognising itself as part of a vast choreography of light.

Let it move you. Let the tiny dances happen. The small turns of the head, the deepening of breath, the tilt of shoulders that feels suddenly right. Trust these impulses; they are your form aligning with currents that hold memory older than any story you have ever told yourself.

There is no need to force revelation. The invisible will come to meet you exactly where you are, speaking in sensations, in pulses, in soft electric murmurs beneath the skin.

And as you allow this dance, without needing to name each step, something opens. The body grows luminous in its own quiet way, not because it has mastered anything, but because it has remembered how to let the unseen flow through unresisted.

This is where the deepest codes land, not through analysis, but through your willingness to be a living part of a mystery that loves you enough to keep inviting you to move.

Chapter Eight

The Holy Animal

You are not just a spirit wearing a body. You are a body that is holy in itself. Muscle and marrow, sweat and salt, all of it luminous with the breath of what made you.

For so long, you were taught to favour the unseen. To trust only what soared beyond gravity, to chase transcendence as if matter was somehow a lesser home. But your bones know better. Your pulse knows better. The quiet insistence of hunger, the thrill that rises unbidden, the tears that fall simply because the heart is too full. These are all proofs of the sacred running through your flesh.

Your body is an animal, yes. It needs warmth, touch, rest, food. It startles at sudden noises, softens under a gentle hand. None of this makes it less divine. It is precisely what roots your light into this world, what lets your soul taste strawberries, feel rain slip down your spine, hear a voice call your name and know it belongs to you.

There is a softness in embracing your holy animal. Not forcing it to perform for worth, not punishing it for faltering, but tending to it as you would a beloved creature. Feeding it well. Letting it sleep.

Stroking its skin with affection simply because it is here, alive, breathing your original light.

When you honour your body this way, you awaken codes that no meditation alone could ever reach. Because it is through this tender tending, this humble caring for the creature you are, that your cells begin to remember they are loved.

And loved cells sing differently. They glow, they open, they speak to each other in clearer patterns. They become better vessels for the luminous architecture of your being.

So pause here. Feel the animal in you, the steady beat of your heart, the warmth of your belly, the slight weight of your limbs. This is not something to transcend. This is a miracle to cherish.

It is here, in this holy animal, that your vastness comes to dwell. It is here that the infinite finds a place to curl up and purr itself to sleep.

Chapter Nine

The Body Remembers

After all the seeking and softening, after the breath and the ache and the tender dance with what cannot be seen, you arrive here, quietly, almost without noticing at the simple truth your body has carried all along. It remembers.

Not as a mind does, sorting through stories and measuring meaning, but as a living field of light woven into flesh. Each cell holds a fragment of your original knowing, tiny lanterns still glowing with the echo of the first breath that ever was.

When you stand still enough, when your thoughts grow hushed and your heart grows tender, you might feel it. The subtle stirrings beneath your skin, the gentle unfurling of something ancient. A familiarity without words. A recognition so deep it trembles through your bones.

This is not memory in the way you've been taught. It is not bound to time or place. It is the remembrance of your wholeness, of your seamless belonging to a vast field of love that never fractured, even when you did.

Your body knows how to return. It was made for it. Every sigh that spills from your lips, every softening of your shoulders, every time you let the tears come without damming them, these are pathways home.

The mind might resist, clinging to patterns that kept you safe once. But your body has always been more honest. It leans toward what feels warm, it opens to what feels kind, it shivers with delight when the light touches it in ways it cannot explain.

Trust this. Trust the holy intelligence of your form. For long after thoughts have run themselves in circles, your body will still be here, faithful, tender, patiently guiding you back to the light it never forgot.

And in this final gentle remembering, you come to rest inside yourself. No longer striving to be more divine, no longer shrinking from your humanness. Simply here. Light woven into matter, matter singing of light.

This is where the journey softens into stillness. This is where you discover that what you sought was never out there, but quietly pulsing beneath your own ribs all along.

The body remembers. And because it remembers, you are already home.

Closing

May these words linger not as thoughts to be dissected, but as a subtle warmth in your chest, a quiet hum beneath your skin.

May your body continue to unfold in its own tender timing, guided by a wisdom older than any story you have ever told yourself.

And when the old ache rises, as it will, not to wound you, but to open you. May you remember that it is only your cells whispering of love, calling you back to the light they have carried all along.

There is nothing left to strive for here. Nothing to prove, nothing to mend. Only this gentle breath, this soft returning, this living body that knows exactly how to find its way home.

Trust it.
It remembers for you.

The Gentle Map

Heart

Sit here and breathe.
What tender ache rises when you let your chest expand without armour?
Let it speak without words.
Feel the warmth or the tightness.
Notice how even the smallest flutter is your heart remembering how to trust.

Throat

Place your hand lightly against your neck.
Feel the delicate flutter beneath.
What truths press forward when you offer them space to tremble?
What have you swallowed that longs to be voiced, even if only as a sigh?

Hands

Rest them open on your lap.
Feel the old impulses to give, to hold, to reach.
What are they longing to touch that has nothing to do with duty?

Let them open wider. Let them rest without grasping.

Belly

Soften here, even if it feels unfamiliar.
Let this be a cradle for all you have ever feared was too much.
Breathe into the warm dark, and notice what unwinds.
Feel how the breath pools here like a quiet lake, asking nothing of you.

Feet

Press them gently into the ground.
Feel the quiet gravity welcoming you.
What would it mean to belong here completely, without hesitation?
Imagine roots growing from your soles, not to anchor you down, but to remind you that you are held.

Back

Lean into whatever holds you: a wall, a chair, the earth.

Notice where you brace, where you yield.
What weight have you carried alone that longs to be shared?
Let the support beneath you whisper: *you do not have to hold it all.*

Shoulders

Roll them gently. Notice how much they carry by habit.
What burden could slip off, even for a breath?
Let them sink away from your ears. Feel the lightness return.

Face

Bring soft awareness here.
What expressions live so long on your skin they have become habit?
Where could you soften, even imperceptibly?
Let the muscles melt, the jaw unhook, the brow ease.

Spine

Trace your awareness slowly from the base of your spine up to the crown of your head.

Feel the quiet electric line running through you.
Where does it flow freely? Where does it catch?
Offer breath to those tender places. Let the current move as it wishes.

Pelvis

Rest your attention in the bowl of your pelvis.
What memory lives here, quiet but insistent?
Can you let this part of you feel safe enough to open, even by a breath?
Trust that it knows how to bloom in its own timing.

Entire Body

Rest in the quiet marvel that you exist at all.
This holy animal of light and bone, breath and ancient memory.
It is here that all your codes land.
It is here that the body remembers what the mind forgets.
Stay as long as you wish.
There is no rush to know.
Only the gentle return.

About the Author

blanche johanna is a writer and sacred scribe whose works are transmissions of remembrance. Through tender, poetic language, she invites souls to soften into the original wholeness that lives beneath all longing.

Her books *The Alchemy of Us*, *The Soul Remembers*, *The Twelve Scrolls*, *The First Light*, and now *The Body Remembers* are living vessels, infused with light codes and gene codes that awaken ancient memory within. Each page bypasses the mind to speak directly to the cells, stirring the deep knowing of who we have always been.

blanche's writing is not offered as teachings, but as gentle activations, a soft return to the light within.

You can explore more of her offerings at www.blanchejohanna.com

www.ingramcontent.com/pod-product-compliance
Lightning Source LLC
Chambersburg PA
CBHW041304240426
43661CB00011B/1008